LEARN ENGLISH

GRAMMER

I0736500

APOLOGIES

Author Lynn Franklin

APOLOGIES

Basic patterns.

I'm sorry. I'm sorry.

I apologize. I apologize. I'm so sorry. I'm so sorry. I'm sorry for criticizing you. I'm sorry for criticizing you. It doesn't matter. It doesn't matter.

I really regret going to the movies last week. I really regret going to the movies last week. I wish I hadn't said that at the party. I wish I hadn't said that at the party. I'm sorry. I I was late for class today. I'm sorry I was late for class today.

You can blame me for this.

You can blame me for this.

I'll take the blame this time. I'll take the blame this time.

Can you forgive me please? Can you forgive me please?

Please accept my apology. Please accept my apology. Can I make this up to you? Can I make this up to you? How can I apologize to you? How can I apologize to you' my fault

There's a lot of traffic in the mornings here.

That's no excuse. You need to give yourself more time to get here.

You're right, sir.

I won't be late again. I hope not. See you tomorrow, bright and early.

dialogue one

I'm sorry, I was late for class

today.

This is the third day this month you've been late.

I know. I know. I'm sorry.

Do you mind telling me why is there something wrong?

Dialogue two.

I thought you said you could finish this report by Tuesday.

I apologize. What can I say?

You almost cost me my job. You were a week late with this project.

Look, I'm sorry. What more do you want?

Do you even have an excuse?

It took more research than I first thought

you could have told me earlier.

I am really sorry. I really messed up. I will try to make this up to you. Okay, I'll give you one more chance.

Dialogue three,

Kim, where were you today? You missed class. I'm sorry. I was feeling ill.

You didn't miss much. It was pretty boring.

Yes, but I already missed class last week to go to the movies.

You might miss too many classes this semester.

I know. I really regret going to the movies last week.

I bet you weren't so sorry then

maybe not then. But I assure him now.

dialogue four

I'm sorry about that last pass. Yeah, that was a pretty bad throw.

I think I need a rest

Is something wrong? Are you hurt?

I hurt my shoulder yesterday.

Well, you shouldn't be playing ball.

You're probably right.

Hey, I'm sorry for criticizing you. I didn't know you were hurt.

It doesn't matter. No problem.

I'll be as good as new and no time. I hope so.

dialogue, five

Debbie, have you seen my red shirt?

Oh, I'm sorry. I forgot to pick up your shirt from the cleaners yesterday.

Well, now I've got nothing to wear to work.

I'm really sorry. I think you've still got the white shirt

I wore that Tuesday. It's pretty wrinkled.

Well, I'll just iron it for you real quick facts. It's the least I can do after forgetting your shirt earlier.

Don't worry about that. Now, honey, at least I've got the white shirt.

Substitution drills.

One

I'm sorry, I was late for class today. I'm sorry. I was late for work today. I'm sorry. I was late for school today. I'm sorry I was late for practice today

two

See you tomorrow, bright and early. See you tomorrow in the morning. See you tomorrow at sunrise. See you tomorrow, early.

Three

This is the third day this month. You've been late. This is the third day this week. You've been late. This is the third day this year. You've been late. This is the third day this semester. You've been late

four

Do you even have an excuse? Do you even have a reason? Do you even have an explanation? Do you even have an alibi?

Five

it took more research that I first thought it took more planning than I first thought it took more preparation than I first thought it took more effort than I first thought.

Six.

Okay, I'll give you one more chance. Okay, I'll give you one more shot. Okay, I'll give you one more opportunity. Okay, I'll give you one more break.

Seven

I really messed up. I really made a mistake. I really heard I really miscalculated.

Eight

I was feeling ill I was feeling not well. I was feeling sick. I was feeling unpleasant.

Nine.

It was pretty boring. It was pretty dull. It was pretty, uninteresting. It was pretty tedious.

10

I'll be as good as new in no time.

I'll be back to normal in no time. I'll be fine in no time. I'll be recovered in no time.

11

Yeah, actually, I hurt my shoulder yesterday. Yeah, actually, I injured my shoulder yesterday. Yeah, actually, I damaged my shoulder yesterday. Yeah, actually I tore my shoulder yesterday

12

well now I've got nothing to wear to work. Well now I've got nothing to put on for work. Well now I've got nothing to dress for work. Well now I've got nothing to throw on for work

13

I forgot to pick up your shirt from the cleaners yesterday. I forgot to get your shirt from the cleaners yesterday. I forgot to grab your shirt from the cleaners yesterday. I forgot to take your shirt from the cleaners yesterday.

14

it's pretty wrinkled. It's pretty dirty. It's pretty stained. It's pretty soiled.

15

Yes, but I already missed class last week to go to the movies. Yes, but I already skipped class last week to go to the movies. Yes, but I already avoided class last week to go to the movies. Yes, but I already ducked class last week to go to the movies.

monologue

Americans put a fairly high value on time. People often eat breakfast while driving to work midday naps during the week are usually only for retired people. People expect appointments to be kept, they expect plenty of notice about upcoming demands on their time. being late or making changes with little notice is acceptable, but some explanation is normally expected.

Many Americans have begun to realize that this concern with time creates stress. However, this realization does little to change most people's habits. In general, Americans believe in the saying that time is money. When time is lost, the belief is that money is also lost. both time and money are often very important in America.

DISCLAMER STATEMENT

All information and content contained in this book are provided solely for general information and reference purposes. SSP LLC Limited makes no statement, representation, warranty or guarantee as to the accuracy, reliability or timeliness of the information and content contained in this Book.

Neither SSP Limited or the author of this book nor any of its related company accepts any responsibility or liability for any direct or indirect loss or damage (whether in tort, contract or otherwise) which may be suffered or occasioned by any person howsoever arising due to any inaccuracy, omission, misrepresentation or error in respect of any information and content provided by this book (including any third-party books.

NOTES

NOTES

NOTES

NOTES

NOTES

NOTES

NOTES

NOTES

NOTES

NOTES

NOTES

NOTES

NOTES

NOTES

www.ingramcontent.com/pod-product-compliance
Lightning Source LLC
Chambersburg PA
CBHW060806210726
48292CB00013B/1900

* 9 7 8 1 9 5 2 5 2 4 6 4 6 *